Formidable Fragility

– NATASHA PENUMUCHI –

An environmentally friendly book printed and bound in England by
www.printondemand-worldwide.com

This book is made entirely of chain-of-custody materials

www.fast-print.net/store.php

Formidable Fragility

Contents

Complex City

No More Coffee

No more coffee
No more tea
No more you deflating
And rejecting me

No more knocking on your door
No more making me feel like a whore
Begging for your attention
Like you're the gate keeper to validate my ascension
To take me up to Heaven's doors

Instead I feel mocked
Less worthy than
Your doormat on the floor

So no more coffee
No more tea
No more you making me feel deflated
No more you rejecting me

I never know what to say
I never know what to do
I feel so low when I am around you
I wish you'd never laid eyes on me
I wish I knew I was out of bounds, so badly
I wish I never went off the rails and wild
Thinking I could handle the fun
Thinking I could be the one to beguile
But no,
As always the tables turned
And I am left with the deep scars and burns
And you're just oblivious
C'est la vie

I don't even like you
I don't know if I even care
But when I'm around you and yours
My spirit feels despair
So instead of fighting
And leaving my lipstick marks on your coffee cups
I shall leave with dignity
Selah Vie

So
No more coffee
No more tea
No more you deflating
And rejecting me

Hazardous

You toxic waste bag
Lying scum bag
Cheating toe rag
I say all this but you're the one I desire
You should wear a warning sign
You're hazardous to all woman kind
Hazardous

How could you just come into my life
Like a thief in the night
Turn my world upside down
Make me have faith in love again
I tried to avoid you
But your scent was too strong

And now...

You toxic waste bag
Lying scum bag
Cheating toe rag
I say all this but you're the one I desire
You should wear a warning sign
You're hazardous to all woman kind
Hazardous

I've been burnt too many times
I should have seen the signs
Maybe I didn't
Because I wanted to believe
That you were different and the Heavens would have mercy on me
Foolish girl
Now I stand here bare
With my heart ripped out and burns everywhere

Why do you have this hold on me?
I keep checking my phone to see if you have called
I have so much to do but arghhhhhhhh!
My mind keeps thinking about you
You're a hazard to my heart
I should have known from the start

You toxic waste bag
Lying scum bag
Cheating toe rag
I say all this but you're the one I desire
You should wear a warning sign
You're hazardous to all woman kind
Hazardous
Yeah, I'm not bitter...

Steal

Take my jewels
Take my phone
Take my body
Yes take it home
Take my pride
But don't steal my joy

Despise my existence
Scoff at my productivity
Cast your stones at my piety
But don't you dare take my peace

Mock me if you will
Like I can stop you
Give me your two pence piece
What you give out saps me dry
But you cannot knock my faith
I'd like to see you try

My confidence does not stem from circumstances
You can't kill my faith with your spears
Though I am wounded by the fiery arrows
Of which are your words
Like a warrior
I press on

Give me riches
Give me gold
Give me the secret of elixir
The prophecies of the ancients foretold
You can give me all this but not in exchange for my peace

For no treasure
No power
No love
No flower
Is worth more than my peace
Nothing is worth more than joy

My choice is to be hopeful
My choice is not to care
My choice is to enjoy the sunshine
Take time to stand and stare
My choice is to be free
Regardless of the inequity

Dangerous Liaison

Favoured Flavour

You're the cream in my coffee
You're the kick in my Saki
You're that tantalising taste when I sink my teeth into a ripe dripping mango
You're a wholesome complex carbohydrate
You're above the need to validate

You tickle my taste buds
You sooth my soul
I feel totally free with you
And out of control

I lie awake and dream of you
My guilty pleasure
I dream of tasting
You're sweet like sugar cane
You are my favoured flavour

You infuse my mind with
Intellectual thoughts
Sending me into fits of excitement

Your fragrance compliments
My sensuality
Our vibes intertwine seamlessly
With intense chemistry
However
Check the sad irony
You do not belong to me
You're the forbidden fruit flavour
The one I so long to savour
But cannot

Bittersweet Elixir

My beautiful nightmare
My picturesque fallacy
My forbidden fruit
My friend
Seeking the truth
My elixir
Bittersweet elixir

My stomach aches with confusion
One minute stimulated with euphoria
Next it's in knots
It turns and shreds
And my heart murmurs and mutters
Yes it mutters

I sit here
Always slightly dismayed
Waiting and praying for that day
Where you will gallantly fall to my feet
And we can finally be

My beautiful nightmare
My picturesque fallacy
My forbidden fruit
My friend
Seeking the truth
My elixir
My bittersweet elixir

Without complication
Can we be free?
To fulfil our desires and needs?
But as I elate myself with this fantasy
You refrain
From wanting me

You've changed your flow
Like the wind you blow
A forceful tornado
Bounding through my mind
And I'm surprised
I cease to be shocked
By the change of your forceful gales
And I'm left to tell my same tale

My beautiful nightmare
My picturesque fallacy
My forbidden fruit
My friend seeking the truth
My elixir
My bittersweet elixir

Statue

If you could only see
The layers of beauty
I have within me
Maybe you won't have to look elsewhere

Maybe if you saw
The bright light
That radiates from deep inside
Then maybe you'll cease
To cast me aside

If only you
Could see me
The way the rest of the world does
Then maybe I won't overwhelm you
Cos you'll see my genuine heart

If you just acknowledge me
The way I do to you
You will finally see
I'm like a statue
Made with rubies, pearls and gold
Maybe then you won't have to be told
How amazing I am
If you just gave me a chance

I often wish and dream
That you would come back to me
I pray for you so lovingly
Even for your family
But am I just fooling myself?
I am strong
But with you I am weak
And you see that when you look at me
So you don't take time to stop and stare
Cos if you did
You wouldn't look elsewhere

If you could only see
The layers of beauty
I have deep within me
Maybe then you'll finally care

If you just acknowledge me
The way I do to you
You will finally see
That I am like a statue

Made with rubies, pearls and gold
Maybe then you won't have to be told
How amazing I am
If you just gave me a chance

I hate loving you the way I do
I try and forget you
But everywhere I go
Reminds me of you
Lord is there a reason for this pain?

My faith is not crushed
Although my heart is
Maybe one day God will bless me
With an astounding man
Someone who will see me
For who I am
Someone who enamours me in every way
This is my heart's desire
Lord I pray

If you just acknowledge me
The way I do to you
Maybe you will finally see
That I'm like a statue
Made with rubies, pearls and gold
Then you won't have to be told
How amazing I am
If you just gave me a chance

Beauty From Ashes

Hung Up My High Heels

I hung up my high heels
I dumped my dating shoes
They gave me too many sores
And I got painfully bruised

Each time I wore my sexy shoes
Thinking my feet would settle and ease through
The same thing happened
Over and over again
It didn't matter where I wore them
The same thing happened, in the end.

So
I hung up my high heels
I dumped my dating shoes
They gave me too many sores
And I got painfully bruised

I wiped off my red lipstick
Pinned up my curly hair
Put down the mascara,
Yes the one I searched everywhere for!
I've folded my clingy clothes
And left my stockings outside the door

And
I hung up my high heels
I dumped my dating shoes
They gave me too many sores
And I got painfully bruised

My girls said try different styles
Maybe even a different shade of blush?
I sighed then said back to them,
"My dear friends
The boys I attract kiss off my lipstick and take off my shoes
Once their done... they leave in a rush".

They don't care if it's flats or heels I wear
Or whether I have a funky flare
So I've decided to plead insanity
Cos I keep doing the same thing
Thinking things will turn out differently

So
I hung up my high heels
I dumped my dating shoes
They gave me too many sores
And I got painfully bruised

But
I missed my red lipstick
And big curly hair
I missed wearing my tight black outfits
I missed the heels I'd wear
Then I realised
I am fine
Just as I am

So now
I wear my high heels
But dumped the dating shoes
And now I'm not singing the dating blues
The red lip gloss is on
I'm joyful
And keep singing my songs

Enough

Inner core
Outer spectrum
The multifaceted human being
Is too cryptic to obtain perfection

Over emotional
Highly vulnerable
Ridiculously seductive
Pseudo strong
Those girls
They speak words of arrogance
From extreme brokenness
That's why their situations always go wrong

Fatal attractions
Leave them incarcerated
Bound
Beguiled
Being knocked inside out

I see these traits concentrated in those girls
But
Then

I too was manipulated by spirits
Which elated and deflated my soul
For so many years
So many tears

Enough
No more
It's not sweet now as it was before
Well
It never really was sweet at all

I was on a quest to obtain
A quest to conquer
I fed my ego
Pseudo nourishment
But I was left
With a more painful hunger

My feelings
Were the centre of my idolatry

However
As I became centred
Vain things, senses, feelings and spirits
That once gratified me so
Divorced themselves from me
Slowly but surely

Old habits became tasteless and harder to follow
New wholesome tendencies
Are now easier acts to swallow
The stress has now left
The bruises are worn away
The scars are disappearing slowly
As my immune system swills and soars

I now have the sound mind
To exhale and release

My Gypsy Dream

My dream is to fly over clouds
So high!

I want to hitch hike over the highlands
And sail over the seven seas
I want to travel through country roads
And admire beautiful streams
I want to sleep under the stars
Travel the nations thus far

I want to feel the warm sand underneath my feet
And march through foreign streets
I am even willing to leave my curling tongs and lipstick at home

But alas
The governing factors that stop me from my adventure
Time and money.

Sanctions On My Sanity

Keep Face

Bitterness is twisted
Resentment is sour
Hatred is dilapidating
Causing erosion in the body
By emotional bile

Injustice
Betrayal
Hard knocks
Can make one frail
The non linear odyssey
Where many angels fear to tread
Sometimes expounds from
Erotic sensations, pseudo relations
That sadly do not lead to the marital bed

Radical thoughts
Imperative ideologies
Often leave me wondering
If our will is truly free?
Are our lives
Orchestrated by the Heavens
Composed like a complex melody?

The more we humble ourselves
And chisel our natural ways
The more blessed we become
Knowing that by self control
We have won

I do not have amnesia
Therefore I won't forget
The tragedies
I've seen
Caused by human greed
And impetuous tendencies

I cannot forget
All the brutality displayed before me
The abuse I've experienced through egotistical control
The violation of my purity by sickly desire
I am wise enough to understand
Not to forget certain matters at hand
How the trusted have ripped me to shreds
The judgement of others left the feeling of dread

But let me not be a victim
And allow past exploitation to consume me so
Let those that have hurt me
Keep face
I'm strong and wise enough
To not be enraged
By their disgraceful folly
It's not up to me to tell them what for
In an emotional erratic manner
For in their perfect arrogance
They'll only feel my weakness

So I plead with you
Let those who stole your heart
The ones who battered you black and blue
Let them keep face
You're better off without them

If you can find it in your heart to forgive
Those who have hurt you
Let them keep face

Ode To Dolly

Ms Dolly Parton
Oh how I admire thee
But I remember you told Jolene
"You can have your choice of men, but I can never love again – he's the only one for me Jolene'
Ms Parton, I love you immensely
And respect you deeply
But just because ladies like me and Jolene
Can have our pick of men
It doesn't mean we captivate their hearts
Or that we're impervious to being broken

It does not mean the men we choose
Will love us true
Most often
Our choice of men
Sweep us off our feet
They drop us from a great height
Again and again

Ms Dolly
You are my heroine
I do not mean to associate you with the drug per se
Although I am addicted to your music
And try to listen to you every day

Ms Parton
You inspire me
My dresses are as short as yours
And I swear we have the same size underwear
But Dolly
I'm unlike you in so many ways
The men I give a piece of my heart to
Enjoy me with great delight
As I get accustomed to the ecstatic sensations
And my whole being starts to defy gravity
A boulder hits me hard
And knocks me right back down to reality

It doesn't surprise me too much
The practice has become quite laborious
What affects me most Ms Parton
Is when they are so uncouth,
Act frightfully ill-mannered
By ignoring me
That's what gets my wick up
That's what aggravates me

Like the song you wrote called *'Little Sparrow'*
That's how the men I like treat me
But like you I am not crushed by them
I am just a broken dream
Fooled by *'cold cross hearted lovers and their evil cunning schemes'*

I believe I must emit a certain scent
That attracts these men of the same ilk

I wish I were like you Dolly
Defiant and strong
I wish I could ask them
Ask them why they did me wrong
Like you did in your precious song

Dear Ms Parton
I feel you understand
You're a *'Backwoods Barbie,*
Too much make up too much hair'
I feel you, Ms Superstar
As I'm from Zone 4
And have been mistaken for a Barbie doll
Too many times before

Like you, my extroversion
And kindness are often misunderstood
My false eye lashes
Pink lipstick
And gold curly hair
Is appreciated in ways that elate and deflate the soul
The goods on the inside
Get cast aside
Most don't see
The rubies, pearls and gold

But Dolly
All is not bleak
Because just like you
I am a Jesus freak
I am controversial
In many ways
But the Lord knows out hearts
And blesses us each day

You write with soul
In your lyrics
You strum with rhythmic excellence
Thanks to you Ms Parton
I can say that I did meet my *'island in the stream'*
But he sailed away to another place
So I cannot rely on him
To be my lover
Anyway I am sad to say
It was all very stealthy and undercover

Dolly Parton
You've got the tongue in cheek
You embody a discerning wise spirit
And have a heart so meek
So here is my ode to you
Mainly to say thank you

You empathise with women like me
Despite the generational gap
We are kindred spirits you see

I pray you continue
To make music so true
And may your formidable legacy
Continue

Anger Management

Okay so I wash everyday
Maybe even twice
And try and look as immaculate as I may
I don't take recreational drugs
And I don't drink alcohol to numb the pain

But I do have addictions
That drives me insane
Like toxic relationships
I've also been addicted to those cancer sticks from time to time
And starving myself didn't help my mind

Right now I am bitter
And I think I have every right to be
Well for now anyway
Even though it just hurts me
To be resentful this way

I am angry that my father didn't invite me to his wedding
And I don't even know my step mothers name.
I am angry that friends I have carried through for several years
Don't even know how to say thank you
I hate that for ten years straight
I have had nothing but heart ache
Go figure

I hate the fact that some men have insulted me
Some even assaulted me
Apparently it's because *'I let it happen'*
I'm sorry if I gave them that impression
All those years ago

I've been a fall back girl
Sadly to the majority
Of the male kind
They say it's because I am a nice girl...

My daddy didn't love me
He beat me incessantly
Then he would buy me gifts and toys
But if he got mad
He'd tell me I was bad
Then take back all the gifts

I have been ridiculed
And called a fool
My name has been slated beyond measure
Why?
I have no idea...
I'm quite quirky
Slightly off beat
I've got more boldness than sense sometimes
Maybe that was why
But regardless of the scoffing
I am destined to succeed

So what if my hair is fake?
And if I gymbox on a daily rate
Who cares if love my red lipstick
Why do people judge and stare?
So what if I want to feed the poor
Empower folks to achieve much more
I believe in human rights
I will stand up and fight!
For that I am fluffy and pink?!

So what if I believe and pray
Am I stupid cos I believe in a deity?
What business is it to you?
And what if I pray for you too?
Why must you slander?
Why must you snide?
Is it to boost your superiority complex?
How pathetic and contrived

You evil freakshow
The type that uses girls
Then call them hoes!
You know full well they love you
Yet you take advantage
Chew them like sugarcane
Suck out the goodness
Then spit them out
When you're done
They lie on the ground
Worthless
Do you care?
No.
Why would you?
You got what you wanted
You gained for what you came
So why are you still empty?
Are you riddled with pain?

Sigh,
Who cares if I am angry?
Who cares if I rant?
Does my heart ache really make a difference?
Maybe
I just need to get some counselling.

Self Harm

Loss of control and anger dwelled inside me
A sense of loneliness
Strong feelings of rejection
And contemplation of suicide
Analytical thought processes consumed my soul
There were points in life where I'd stick my fingers far down my throat
In order to feel a sense of control
It was my dark way of taking initiative over what I hated to see
I demonically actualised my fantasies
Through the pain
I hoped that they would come true
Left in an atrocious state of discontent
That was then
A decade a go
But if I didn't tell anyone
No one would have known
Sylvia Plath Syndrome
That was the disease I had
All those years ago

And now
So much has been accomplished
And more to be achieved
Opulence is to obtained
And destiny is to be fulfilled
The journey of healing
Has taken its course already
Faith has and continues
To fill that void deep within
The comfort of the Holy Spirit
Strengthens me

But as I drive my overly ambitious ego
My diligence and wellbeing are left behind
I drive so fast on my road to nowhere
That there are no signs to read
And I am back
To those feelings of self hatred and despair
Back to feeling rejected and useless
And back to those thoughts that nobody cares

Formidably fragile
As tears roll down my face I still smile
I am a rock to many and an angel to most
I really don't mean to sit here and boast
But as I dwell in my dark place
I ask the Lord above who is full of grace
Do angels cry?
And do they hurt?
Do they feel mistreated?

Alas, I am no angel
But I've been blessed beyond belief
A wise man once said
'The greater the light, the greater the heat'
I believe that is so

Out of brokenness
I speak arrogant phrases
And sing self elating songs
When really
It is plain to see
Regardless of how formidable my character may be
I long to be loved by my Prince Charming
Is this just an ideology?

I find it hard sometimes
To stomach throwaway statements
They cut me like a knife
They hurt me
Just like I used to hurt myself
Knives, scissors and cut!

The mind is a battlefield
Psychological blocks
Hinder my progression
Meditation and focus are imperative
To work through my roller coaster of emotions
Now when I breakdown in tears
I'll take it to the Lord in prayer
And cease to self harm.

Justified Injustice

Cast Your Stones

Cast your stones
All you Pharisees
Lift and throw
And hide me under the debris

Spit your venom at my innocent face
Burn with anger
Be inflamed with your disgrace at me
Go ahead and judge me
Make up accusations that coincide with your malignant understanding
All because I do not follow the notes and rhythm
Of your orchestration
I have got my own melody

Therefore whatever I do
To show you I care
You reject
As it isn't organised by you
That's why you ridicule and stare
Your martyrdom is a *pharse*
As it's controlled by nervous energy
Your dictatorship is commendable
You are formidable to say the least

Your intellect is astounding
So sharp that you often cut yourself
Your world...well now, is not mine
Even though I would be there to see you every single state and kind

I would console your cries and your woes
I would even trek across mountains and rivers to be with you so
To help give me a break and you a sense of love
I have even carried you in my thoughts and prayers
But when it was my turn to be ripped apart by life's hardships
You turned away.

Sometimes

Dear Dad,
I never really did understand you
Although many times I tried
I tried to see why you did what you did
Why you made me feel
Like I wanted to die

Why did you do all the things?
I pray to the Lord above
I ask him to forgive me
As I find it so hard
To forgive you
For all the hell you put me through
And this is really something
I need to do

But sometimes I wish you loved me
Sometimes I wish you tried
That you acknowledged my existence
Instead you just made me cry
I really should forgive you
Sometimes I try
Sometimes

It's your fault why my body's this way
Because your controlling ways
It's your fault you weren't there for me
That's why I choose men who disregard me
It's your fault that I find it hard
To value who I am
If you were man enough
Things would have gone to plan

Instead you almost killed me
With your fists and your words
You broke my confidence
It just doesn't make sense
Why you have rejected me so
When you don't know who I am
I don't mean anything to you
Is this part of God's plan?

Sometimes I wish you loved me
Sometimes I wish you tried
That you acknowledged my existence
Instead you just made me cry
I really should forgive you
Sometimes I try
Sometimes

I'm taking this in my stride
Undoing all the wrong you did
And now I'm trying to
Do things right
I know you're not all bad
You have your bitter story too
I just wish we could have gone through it together
Instead I feel misused

But God bless you on your journey
I pray you finally have peace
I pray your soul has no more turmoil
And that your sleep is sound
I know I will be fine
As I have my beautiful mother and friends
And I have my Lord Jesus on my side

But sometimes I wish you'd loved me
Sometimes I wish you'd tried
That you'd acknowledged my existence
Instead you just made me cry
I really should just forgive you
That's what I'm gonna do
Put an end to my misery
And let God see me through.

The Waiting Game

Each day I am held captive by my thoughts
Each day I break in silent cries
I am waiting on promises
It seems God, you've forgotten my cries
My cries of brokenness
Cries of woes
Cries of deep heartbreak that nobody knows

I am grateful; please do not get me wrong
I live in gratitude, that is why I sing my songs
But please Lord, remember me
As these visions, dreams, thoughts and desires
Are starting to hurt me
Each time I feel this
I realise how weak I am
Each time my heart yearns

I reach out to the solid rock
I reach out because I don't want to be swept away again
I don't want to be so caught up that I'm drowning in my tears and misery
Dear God
I pray for tenacious spirit that endures the storm
Please Lord don't let me not build my dreams on sand
But on the solid rock on which I can stand
And get through the knocks and raging sea
Regardless of the hard hits
Let my mind be strong to hold on
To the truth
And your promises

But while I hold on
With all my strength and my might
Please Lord, see the way in which I fight
Give me courage and strength
Give me revelations before I faint
As my faith goes beyond reason
And my dreams beyond current fact
I pray you answer my cries
I pray you send angels to dry my eyes
It seems like all I do is battle all day long
I am waiting for the day when I sing my song
Of praise as I stand in the dream
As I receive the desires of my heart
And watch my prayers unfold
Materialise into reality
Lord I pray for that day
That's what keeps my sanity

Imprisoned

I am chained
I am bound
My mind is a slave to the system
No matter how I wish to break free
Finances keep me imprisoned

Angels In Training

I Wish

Right now, I do not wish for glamour and fame
Although those things would be grand.
At this moment, I do not wish for the 5 star treatment.
I don't even want sun, sea, sky or sand!
I'm not even fussed about being successful. I know one day I will be.
Today I am not worried about money because with diligence I know it won't leave me

Now I wish for strength and emotional stability
I wish to walk around as if I do not have a care in the world
Regardless of my circumstances slowly breaking me.
Even though I am transparent
I have nothing to hide–people can see right through me.
I wish, like Miss Vic Martin I had the strength to give and love regardless

My simple thoughts and basic rhymes may not impress the masses or entertain in kind
But sometimes maybe simple thoughts and simple words
Encourage more perspective
And it makes my voice... Well, heard!
I know I should not worry, I know I should not care.
Instead I must take everything to the Lord in prayer
I still find it amazing,
When people pass by
How they hold it all together
You would think that they didn't even cry

In dark times, they radiate beams of light
I wish I could be like that
Instead I break down and cry

I'm a vocalist in every sense of the word
I vocalise my thoughts, feelings and impressions
I vocalise my joy and my hurt
But sometimes you can communicate better
In silence and stillness
When not a word can be heard.

I miss Pastor Renato
So much, I never knew how much I would miss someone like that
You see
It's been one year since the day he died
From that dreaded cancer
But I praise God he is in Heaven now
And has the Lord by his side

I understand people drift in and out of our lives like seasons
But some are there for the duration
I do not want to be so busy
That I forget who is around me and has allowed me to be me
I do not want time to drift by so fast
That I only see my loved ones when
I am following a hearse!

Sad as it seems, morbid as I may sound
That is the type of life I sometimes lead
So it is time for me to take heed

I wish to have strength like Miss Vic Martin
Courage like Usha Penumuchi
And faith like Theresa Emmanuel
It is time for me to pray like Natasha Awuku
And care like Keely Augustus

It is time for me to be focused like James Cassim
And be a rock like Carla Netto
It is time for me to be brave like Jade Kellman
And to take a stand like Rasha Abdul Rahim
It is time for be to be grounded like Najwa Saleh
And endure like Helen Sharma and Auka Ansah

I wish I could believe like my mummy
And be bold like Suresh Oliver
I wish I could be spirited like Patricia Da Silva
Have compassion like Natalie Letch
Integrity like Karan Bangera
And be sincere like Leon Fenner
I wish to be creative like Isi Adeola
Wise like Sima Jaan
And humble like Mel Canning
I wish to have passion like Nargess Moballeghi
I wish to embrace the life I have and not sit here and mourn

I wish
I wish
I wish!

My Rock

To Princess Carlita of Omelette Land

My rock
My friend
From the age of 11 until grave's end
My blessing from God
My militant angel
Sent from the Heavens above
To be there for me through absolutely everything
From the great tragedies
To listening to the new songs I've written
And those I'm ready to sing

My Gibraltarian rock
Which I lean on
Small and petite
But Lord have mercy
The strength of Carlita can contend with Samson

I can pick up the phone and not say a word
She will know every emotion I am experiencing
Just like that
Without a moment to spare
She is by my side
Allowing me to laugh and cry

In times of despair
Anxiety and fear
We call upon each other
To laugh and cheer
Embrace life with a smile and strength
To react to heartache with one liners
Banter that raises us further up
Than a step incliner.

I love you precious girl
You make my heart sing
Because no matter how life hurts you
You'll always do the right thing!

Peace to you x

Radiant

She may not seem much from afar but right up close she glistens like a
star.
She's so radiant, beautiful and radiant.
She may be hard to perceive as her motives are pure and her nature
is sweet, she's so radiant, beautiful and radiant.

I can't believe she's been abused before; she says men have walked
over her and headed straight out the door.

And I see tears in her eyes, as she tries not to cry...

Still she holds her head up high and loves beyond boundaries of sun,
sea and sky; she's so radiant, beautiful and radiant.

She may not seem much from afar but right up close she glistens like a
star
she's so radiant, beautiful and radiant.

She may be hard to perceive as her motives are pure and her nature
is sweet, she's so radiant, beautiful and radiant.

She seems to be bitter free and lives a selfless life with integrity; she's
so radiant, beautiful and radiant.

This is for the ladies who've held on to their dreams despite the pain
they've held within-you're all so beautiful, so awesome and beautiful.

This is for the people who make the most of life despite the hurt and
crashes; they've risen up strong, beauty from ashes, beauty from
ashes.

She may not seem much from afar but right up close she glistens like a star
she's so radiant, beautiful and radiant.

You may not think you're much from afar but deep inside you know you're a glistening star: You're radiant, beautiful and radiant.

Dedicated to Usha Penumuchi, Keely Augustus, Carla Netto and Helen Sharma.

Yo Kellmanovich

An Ode to Spaghetti by Natasha Penumuchi (Meatball)

When you feel sad
When you feel blue
Just remember Meatball loves you

Life has a funny way of bringing us down with stresses and strains
But we just have to sit back and remember our Darwin days
Oh we were so blind, we really couldn't see
We thought we were doing a good service to the UKC community

The days when we stole... and ran away
The day you turned a straight hot man gay
The day we saved Jim's life 'Red Duct Tape'
The day you took *The Scream* out on a date

The days we guzzled beers galore
The days we used to sit and watch ... (*just let yourself go Joe*)
The days when Mr J Silk argued with us and tied our bras to each others doors
The day I got thrown out of the Venue club and you landed on the floor

Your multicoloured Rasta hat was your trademark
You with your *Red Label* tea and me and my batty riders
We knew from then, there was a spark
The days we lived on pasta and rice
The days we strutted round the Venue, all voluptuous, thinking 'we're too nice!'
The days of me trying to straighten your biff, which proved to be a nightmare
The day Adrian creamed his leg on my table; now that gave us all a scare
The days we cried to each other about life
The days you used to scream about the dishes; at times I thought you were my nagging wife!

From you falling over at many points, too many times too mention
To me wearing statement makeup thinking I was getting all the boys' attention
You used to read *The Sun* to me without fail
I used to practice my singing and the neighbours threw a can at me that nearly broke the bathroom rail

The days we'd used to film ourselves doing random things
The days I used to go straight to church from a night of debauched partying
The days when we were rich and we were poor (not much changes there)
To now, where we are screaming; oh my gosh! We are 24!!!!

Our endless quotes and self praises:

'Hot-Not'
ebay? Sick bay!
FIVE POUND
What did the 5 fingers say to the face?
To war
You maybe spaghetti, but I'm noodles!
Am I buff? Yes! Do I care? No!
ConFIdence

A picture of my face being put on a dart board
You falling into your wardrobe
You starting fights with everyone and me pouring Snake Bite down them
You're the vegetarian that likes to eat meat.

Our friendship did not end there
We continued to have jokes and grew to look even buffer and oh so fair
You being hostile to the security guard because I lost my phone for the 100th time
Us trekking through Stonebridge, a place you love so dear!
Every time I see you; I cannot help but laugh, cry, cuss and laugh some more.

Dude I'm here for you through thick and thin
Through the expansion and decreasing of waistlines and the confessions of all our sins
Through the Matts, Pratts, and the list could go on
(Hope it doesn't too much otherwise that would be... Er, ERROR!!)

I hope you like my cheesy poem; it made me laugh and cry.
The friendship of Spaghetti and Meatball will always live on
It's a great combination and its unity will never die.

Although we may get paired up with different kinds
Like Naan bread, Bolognaise, Potatoes and Veg
There's nothing quite like Spaghetti and Meatball – as we've got the edge ;-).

Love you forever!

My Angel

For my darling Uncle Romy
May he rest in peace!
'Now I lay me down to sleep
I pray the Lord and my soul to keep me
From crying
And let the angels watch me through the night as I wake in the morning light'
Amen

There was a man who had a heart like gold
Who was more compassionate and sacrificial than
Any fictitious character in previous stories told
He was the firstborn

He was the echelon of society
Had a formidable mother
Beautiful siblings
His father was amazing on the outside
But ghastly within
His dad was a Major General indeed
So everyone had to march to his beat

Romy had everything yet nothing
He had nothing yet had everything
The apple of everyone's eye
Did all he could to help the family survive
Survive the shame, survive the pain
Of what his father did to them

Romy's heart and credentials
Were in the right place
But squandered and wandered throughout the East
He rose and fell dozens of times
In the midst of Mecca and on Chennai's streets

Although his flesh
Burned with the desire
For instant gratification
Yearning for the demon drink that fuelled
An evil fire
However, his soul was still sweet
Countenance still pure
He would give up everything
To help you off the floor

He prayed to God so sweetly
And never denied Jesus for earthly gains
Not many people
I know would refrain
From such worldly promotions
But Uncle Romy did
Because deep in his heart
He knew Heaven would forbid

He did the right thing in malaprop ways
He drove his loved ones mad
So where we'd shout in a great craze
But what can you do
When Uncle Romy came to you with all his issues
It broke our hearts
To see his body deteriorate
In such a heartrending manner
But his spirit was so strong
Saying all will be fine tomorrow
Tomorrow
Tomorrow
Was what he'd say

Without fail he'd call me Angel
From the day I was born
Until the last time he called
My heart breaks
My body in pain
Two days after I received the news
I'm grief stricken

I always had an idealised view of my sweet Uncle Romy
But I saw too much
When I was in India last
It made me so mad
And thought back to my past
I was so angry that he let himself
Be destroyed
From a former gentleman
To a man begging for money
To buy his son toys

I wanted him to stand on his own two feet
And be the best he could be
I wanted him to prove everyone wrong
But then when he died
It was too late.

His interesting life of dark tales and woes
Leaves one to wonder can this man go straight through to Heaven's doors?
But Uncle Romy's heart was so pure.

He is a true inspiration to me
Not because he had riches galore
Not because he wasted opportunities
Handed to him on a plate
Not because of his dodgy dealer ways
But because he had a good word to say
About everything and everyone.

He wouldn't be malicious
Or have a snake-like tongue
He would prefer to hurt himself than hurt you
He stood by his faith
He smiled and laughed
And was so honest and true

He called me his Angel
Although I am far from it
From the time I was born till the time he passed
He called me his Angel
But now he is mine

As I sit here and write this ode to my inspiration
I wail and cry
Deeper than I have cried before
For he has taught me such a lesson
That I cannot ignore

He taught me to be still and know that there is a God
To be kind even when it is hard
To honour even when you want to kill
To be loving even when you are hurt
He taught me to be honest about who I am
And enjoy life to the full
But from his mistakes I have learned
To not give up on my dreams
To not give in to demonic addictions
Or things that cause pain and affliction.

Thank You

Dedicated To Usha Penumuchi aka Mummy

Chief Editor: Lory Frenkel
Editor: Bridghe Ford
Graphic Designer: James Cassim
Photographer: Helen Boast

ND - #0158 - 080726 - C0 - 210/148/4 - PB - 9781780350639 - Gloss Lamination